ELEMENTAL

Denise Thompson-Slaughter

Plain View Press
P.O. 42255
Austin, TX 78704

plainviewpress.net
sb@plainviewpress.net
512-441-2452

Copyright © 2010 Denise Thompson-Slaughter. All rights reserved under International and Pan-American Copyright Conventions. No part of this book may be reproduced or distributed in any form or by any means, or stored in a data base or retrieval system, without written permission from the author. All rights, including electronic, are reserved by the author and publisher.

ISBN: 978-1-935514-19-0
Library of Congress Number: 2010934407

Cover art: *Irises and Sun Mandala*, by D. Otto Conner.
Cover design by Susan Bright.

for Tom—

my rock, my mirror—

and for

the late John Duffy,

who believed in me first

Acknowledgments

I am grateful to the editors of the following journals for first publishing these poems:

"Blessing," *Friends Journal*, Nov. 2007;
"Blind Creation," *Visions International*, 2009;
"Calendar" (two single verses) *Raw Nervz Haiku* (Canada), Winter 2001 and Summer 2001;
"Certain Illnesses," *Karamu*, Spring 2005;
"Chaos Verde," *Tucumcari Literary Review*, Aug. 1999;
"Civil War," *Rockhurst Review 2008: A Fine Arts Journal*, 2008;
"Einstein's Not Here," *U.S. 1* newspaper (Princeton, N.J.), July 28, 1999;
"Flotsam," *The Plowman* (Canada), Nov. 2000;
"Forage," *Friends Journal*, Aug. 2005; "'G' is for Gone," *A Different Latitude*, Deleware Valley Poets, 1999;
"Happy Ending" *Mother Muse* anthology, ed. Sueann Wells, 2009;
"Hyper," *Rockhurst Review 2007: A Fine Arts Journal*, 2007;
"The Listing Wife" *Quantum Tao* 3, Summer 1998;
"Mayflies," *ByLine*, May 2007;
"Nightwatch," *California Quarterly*, May 2004;
"Some Grace," *Mother Muse* anthology, ed. Sueann Wells, 2009;
"The Subdivision," *Earth's Daughters*, 2007;
"Traces," *TOWER poetry* (Canada) Winter 2002–03.

Contents

earth   7
  Nightwatch   9
  The Subdivision   10
  Reconciliation   11
  Haiku for Willie   15
  Calendar   16
  The Nature of the Beast   18
  The Door   19
  "G" is for Gone   20
  The Scales of Love   21
  Blessing   22
  Spider   23
  Summer's Edge   26
  Duet for Two Hands: Lilith and Eve   27
  Mama's Shadow   29
  Mud Wrestling   30

water   31
  Chalice   33
  Deliverance   34
  Shifting   35
  Flotsam   37
  When Lobstermen Were Lawyers   38
  Pastille: Bay of Fundy   39
  Oasis   40
  Spring Babble   41
  Lost   42
  Maroon   44

fire   45
  Best Foot   47
  The Aging Poet   48
  Palette   49
  Hyper   50
  Advanced Attachment   51
  A Glass Darkly   52

She Said	53
Certain Illnesses	55
Civil War	56
Traces	57
Slow Melt	58
Sitting Shiva	59

air   61

Blind Creation	63
Einstein's Not Here	65
Indulgence in Infrared	66
Mayflies	67
Happy Ending	68
Northern Cross	69
In the Editors' Diner	70
Caged Canary	71
Sprung	72
Reverie	73
Take These Broken Wings	74
Chaos Verde	75

spirit   77

Altaring	79
Inventory	80
Call Me Al	81
Splintered Symphony	83
The Listing Wife	84
The Hindu Quaker	88
Meditation	89
Recycled	90
Some Grace	91
The Gift	92
Forage	93

About the Author   95

EARTH

Nightwatch

Midnight: I turn off my lamp.
Your small snores shift, sighing into darkness.
One child is restless, tossing in the arms
of a metal bunk;
the other sleeps on soft carpet beside her bed,
the sweetness of her slumbers hovering in the air
like a mist-filled cocoon.

I have this need
to be the last consciousness in the house.
Someday I will want to remember:
I bore witness to this susurration of breath
in the dark hallways of each night,
soothing sounds like the red-shifting trace of traffic
down the hill
or the serenade of cicadas and crickets
filtering through our bedroom window.

The Subdivision

As children in a barren land,
bored in our naked new houses,
we foraged the mounds of red Maryland clay
for bottles left by construction workers.

Up on the highway, at the Enterprise Bar and Carry-out,
we were paid a nickel apiece: legal ransom for the glass
from a man whose time we were wasting
while we chose our ten-cent snacks.

One Saturday, land scoured bare of bottles,
we went beyond the raw Martian landscape,
past the fringe of trees where the
ponderous tread of bulldozers
had not yet left their zig-zag tracks,

found crumbled foundations of an old plantation:
another country, right out of our history books.
"Slave quarters!" we whispered nervously
as we stumbled over each new ruin.

For we were just below the Mason-Dixon
line of ancestral shame.
Was Maryland ever really the Old South?
In skittish silence, we explored,

fearing the vengeful ghosts of slaves—
and masters, too,
who would not like their history plowed under by bulldozers
or pillaged by children.

We found only the terrible bones of cattle:
such fearful treasures
as could not be traded for nickels or candy.

Reconciliation

A memory:
Laughter echoed up the stairwell
to my small apartment.
"Damn! Dropped it again!"
Male giggles.
My father and his brother,
drunk again,
trying to deliver the sofa
I had inherited
from parental reconciliation—
the first of three;
Next time, I'd get Mom's TV,
and in one piece, too.

It had taken a moment
to recognize the drunken commotion as mine—
coming to me—
a pale green velour sofa
finally arrived on the second floor
minus two legs
that leaped off in all the hilarity.

"You have plenty of books!" he said,
disdain leaking out like the odor of stale beer.
"Prop it up on them!"
I did.
It worked.
The sofa had a skirt
so her legs didn't show.

Like me. My books didn't show either,
because he'd always said,
"You don't want to be too smart.
 The smart ones always go crazy.
 Look at your aunt.

11

  And look at all the famous writers
    and geniuses—they're always crazy!"

By that first day of my adulthood,
when my paternal ogre came into focus
as an arrested adolescent
and I became
the proud owner of a crippled couch,
I'd already discovered
that men fell for my space-cadet act.
Keep your books under your skirt
until you're sure you're on stable ground.

Twenty years later,
after Reconciliation III,
my mother lay dying in a room of her own,
having just bought a three-bedroom townhouse
as an act of bold denial.

I drove the 200 miles, settled in
to a room with the Seven Dwarves
painted on the wall.
Bashful was always hard to find,
hiding behind the nightstand; but
when Mom called out
in the middle of the night,
I took comfort in the solid
beneficence
of Doc's bespectacled face,
before facing the feces
or vomit
or just utter confusion
of someone who didn't even know she'd called,
much less why.

In the whitewashed light of each March morning,
even before the fool woodpecker

began drilling the aluminum gutter,
my father would leave his little blue room
and tiptoe down to make coffee.
Although I asked him not to,
he woke me up as soon as it perked.
"Coffee's ready!" really meant:
"Wake up and tell me if she's still alive.
 I'm too scared to look for myself."

But he was so grateful
it was worth a few more hours' lost sleep.
Slowly we became friends.

Mom never called for his help but once,
after I pleaded with her to let him feel needed.
All of her deathbed confessions to me
were indictments of his life:
the time he slept with a prostitute,
the time he went to jail drunk and disorderly,
the horrible stories about
his father's abuse of the badge.

After it was all over,
Dad spent every evening sitting in her empty room
talking to her until it was too dark to see
the pink ruffled bedspread,
the untouched vanity,
the photos on the white wall.

In this way, two years drifted by.
After his first stroke,
he forgot the previous three decades
and had to grieve all over again
for his lost health,
his mother, brothers, and

the young wife he remembered
so alive and well.

Now, as clouds of smoke and
years of beer
clog his arterial byways and
lay claim to diabetic digits,
he lets nothing distract him from his mission:

Waiting
without his toes
for the next reconciliation.

Haiku for Willie

After our dog died,
the foghorn tolled for a week.
Summer felt like fall.

I remember how
his big head lay in my lap.
Bagged and hauled away.

Returned in a box:
ashes beneath an ash tree.
I wished for dogwood.

Calendar

Rivers race to sea.
A gull surfs on branch-boat prow.
Bold April struts in.

Splashing of spring rain.
Lightning rips across the sky.
I think of your arms.

The sun came on strong
when the rain and fog lifted.
Everywhere, steam rose.

A year of extremes:
now we are praying for rain.
The red clay sprouts cracks.

Parched throats ache with thirst.
Heat shimmers on a black road.
Grass gives up the ghost.

Pigeons pecking ants,
scratching on the dust-dry earth.
Rain drops, blessing all.

Autumn treasures come:
azure skies, jewel-toned leaves and
berries, ripe and plump.

Children in new clothes
call out to one another
as they traipse to school.

Cobblestones beneath
a yellow-leafed canopy:
campus in autumn.

Underfoot, dry leaves;
passing geese honk above us.
Our breath hangs on air.

In perfect stillness
delicate snowflakes muffle earth:
radiant cold night.

Icicles dripping
as bright sun warms mid-day roof.
Rainbows on the wall!

The Nature of the Beast

Three dogs—a brown, a black, a white—
consecutive canines,
all loved so
that I thought I could never love another.

But love is like that.
It sneaks in the window
even when you know you've closed the door.
And thank God!
And thank Dog.

You know you felt that way about your children:
as if you could never love another
more than the baby you held in your arms,
whose soft sweet-smelling head seemed to be ever so subtly
      molding itself to your shoulder.
But of course you were washed with the same swell
 of emotions when you held the next one.

Yet dogs are much less complicated than children;
and their love is unconditional,
the way we wish ours were.
But then,
that is the difference
between us
and God
and dogs.

The Door

With a creak of hinges,
the door closed: heavy, final,
echoes reverberating with my defiant "NO!"
On the stoop, pounding the door in grief,
I stood.
A stranger with a small dog
watched sympathetically as I wailed.

Well do I know the sound of death in my dreams.

But in life it arrives
with so little fanfare.
Not the shadow of a raven
darkens the sunlight where we sit—
reading, perhaps, as we wait for the doctor
or for the patient to wake and say,
"Are you still here?"

"G" is for Gone

My mother died
as I was reading
the penultimate chapter
of a Sue Grafton novel.
Only I was there.

Kinsey Millhone was reckless, as usual,
in the face of grave danger—
mysteries were my mind's anchor through
      that dark spring
until I found a greater mystery chained to my ankle:
How could I have been so careless
as to miss the sudden cessation of breath?
the shimmer of her rising spirit in the morning sun?
Only the alarmed face of the young nurse,
stopping by on her first round,
caused me to put down my book
and wonder to this day
on what page death pounced.

The Scales of Love

"He loves you as much as he is able"
the fortune cookie said.
Oh, years ago.
It lay there on the table,
quickly covered by my cloth.

I was stricken, yet I knew it true.
From what was *I* protecting *you*?

Now you turn cold, withdraw
      to lick raw grief,
as I count loss upon loss
and watch old wounds open and bleed, despair
a hungry loanshark behind me.

Both houses hit by depression,
I find no counterweight to hang in the balance.
Your account mislaid
in this bug-infested bank of mutual trust,
      I love you
           as much as I am able.

Blessing

Too swift, time robs me of my very thoughts;
dreams stay unexamined
       and soon forgotten; tiny images dart now and then,
here and gone, here
fragments peck like crows
       then fly off before I can befriend them.

But oh the compensations!

Those little hands; that smile; the
screams of delighted discovery; spontaneous hugs:
tiny arms wrapped tight around my knees,
       standing at the kitchen sink;
the bedtime dance;
that bow-legged stance toddling away—
   soft dark curls and the
   yellow-ribboned balloon bobbing obediently behind!

Before *you*: trillions of thoughts, decades of dreams
wait
like Christmas presents newly wrapped in the attic,
       to be discovered in time.
A few dark lumps of grief inside the stocking, no doubt,
       but (I pray)
mostly bright and shiny,
       rainbow-hued
            boxes full of joy for you.

Spider

Mice we catch with kindest trap
and take them to the woods.
Bigger than some mice are,
you would never have fallen
for a bit of peanut-butter bait.

I warned you, I did,
even gave you twenty-four hours' notice.
A creature that big and scary in my laundry room
cannot be.
I tried to communicate,
fancied I felt your alien mind
sizing me up, you,
scared but not cowed,
dry, cynical, whispery, flat sort of thinking.
It made me uncomfortable
instead of familiar.

"I would have killed it," said the man of the house,
trying to decide if I was funny
or insane for attempting telepathy with spiders.
"A spider that big, I would've killed."

I thought about my clothes drying
on the rack, my nightgowns on the rails,
the bites I've been getting.
Oh, Shelob, Mother of All Spiders,
how many are your spawn?
The spring increase of resident spiderlets:
generations of your kin?
I thought about my Little One,
allergic to so much;
what would a spider bite do
to her reactive little body?

When next we meet,
my heart skittles to the pit of my stomach.

I warned you, I whine,
hairs rising on the back of my neck.
You peek out from behind the pipe
as if that slender stalk of two-inch metal
can hide your enormous body on a white wall.
I pick up the dustpan
reluctantly,
edge you—reluctant, too—a few inches toward the sink,
knock you in,
fumble hurriedly with the tap;
the handle, broken sharp by a careless painter's wrench,
hurts my hand when I try to turn it.

I settle for cold water—slower, crueler, I know—
and the tub won't fill quickly enough.
Your long legs, thick as twigs, mottled with black,
touch bottom and race for sink wall.
With dustpan full of water
I dish you back, again and again,
thinking, oh, this is too slow, too cruel,
torture, but still I'm loathe to confront
a splat of such magnitude.
I don't know if it's physically possible
to squelch a spider the size of a mouse;
I realize anyway you're too big for the drain.
Panic rising, I turn my weapon on edge
and try to hack you in half, ending it quickly;
but you're tough and moving and
I get only a couple of those terrible legs.
We both watch with horror as they float down the drain.
A few more strikes and you're out, down the hole,
carried along through pipes under the street
on your way to Water Treatment and the final resting place
of martyred spiders.

What would the Dalai Lama say?
I close my eyes now and see,
in a wash of red, the wriggling, teeming, crawling things
that probably live in the foundations,
suddenly freed from their fear of the Spider Queen.
Did she keep us safe from these?

Maybe she could have been trapped by tupperware,
taken upstairs and thrown out a window,
loosened lid flying off, freeing her
to make her way in the wide world
outside my laundry room.
Maybe next time.

Summer's Edge

Children milk September evenings,
squeeze the last drops of summer from the shadows beyond sunset,
pushing the new school year out, over the edge of thought
with bikes and balls and games
that take on a new intensity with the waning of the day,
just as the chorus of cicadas crescendo before the seasons change.

Parents emerge from stuffy houses,
wiping their hands on dish towels
      or eyeing their lawns with rue.
They sit on stoops, cluster on sidewalks
        to catch the breeze;
        to wonder when the weather will break;
        to predict the play-off results or the cool front
            coming from Canada,
        then announce the countdown until bath and bed.

Washed in lilac light punctuated by the first flicker
      of street lamps,
exhausted tykes begin to self-destruct in tiny mishaps or tears.
Their sticky bodies are carried inside, wailing,
as older children are picked off by ones and twos,
called to the burden of homework by reluctant but tired parents who,
sighing in the last breeze, put their shoulders to the wheel
while wishing they could stay outside and play.

Duet for Two Hands:

Lilith and Eve

The nails were never any good
but once my hands were beautiful.
My best friend told me so in high school
as she plotted to get pregnant
by my boyfriend
so she could get away from home.

I was surprised to see my hands that way,
as her hand too surprised me
every time she dealt.
A joker in every round; was it me or her?

I tried to protect her then, but later
when the body count rose,
I judged her harshly. Too harshly
perhaps.

She hated herself, pursued
a dozen self-destructive paths.
Some crossed mine,
opened holes in my life
where lovers and friends used to be.

Yes, Virginia, there is intentional malice in the world;
my eyes opened to the poker games, the chess,
the Russian roulette
that we play with one another.
I folded: worked, studied, licked my wounds,
married, remarried, and moved far away.
I thought of her only when I considered my hands.

And now my fingers bleed every winter,
cracks opening in parched clay,

red-rimmed crevices sting knuckles and thumbs,
dried up, like the canals on Mars
where we scratch to make a living
         in the dust outside the gates.

Mama's Shadow

I labor to
track out of this
dark forest
not just for fear
of phantom-haunted trees
or again to feel the breeze-
spun sun on my face,
but most of all
for the sake of
those small sprites
who lurk on the edges.
My fear draws them in
even as I want them to
fly free.

Be not comfortable here,
nor make this wood
your own!
Heart-spawn
full-sprung
imps of my own
pining.

Mud Wrestling

"Let your heart dwell in the house of love,"
some part of me whispers to myself,
as I feel the strings of anger tighten my chest,
weaving a web, invisible but sticky,
      to trip me again.
Breathe.
I receive the mantra
in the garden of my soul
and try to convince it to take root there.
Grow, blossom, bear a fruit called contentment
amid folded gold-veined leaves of patience.
One day at a time,
sometimes hour by hour, minute by minute,
I wrestle to keep it alive,
only to find myself face down in the mud three out of five
throws. Sow
again.
How else can I survive this week, this month, this year,
      this motherhood,
           marriage,
                mayhem,
                      disappointment,
                            life,
                                death?

They will break my heart a thousand times,
And I will sow again.

(But possibly I'll need to pull up some stakes.)

WATER

Chalice

Poetry has no reason.

It is the welling-over,

the bubbling at the lip,

where subconscious

surges up

into consciousness.

Deliverance

A gentle rain
in the bittersweet desert of solitude
you came.

A sound reaching
where every tongue had become alien.

A pyramid
in the shifting sands of confusion and self-doubt,
where reality had always turned into
betrayal,
and sanity
a philosophical term
bandied in the winds of fear.

Now
saltpan, oasis,
sheiks and scorpions
fade.
You are here.
Life is yet to be lived.

Shifting

                    Kiss of foam ices my
              too-long confined city toes,
      sighing, plashing, each sea-breeze breath
                  soothing away,
              numbing the past year.

   By frost this beach will seem a distant dream;
      this land, far away, beyond my mortal reach.

But when again we roll off the ferry
to gull calls,
rag-tag rigs,
tumbled piles of traps and flaking orange buoys,
smell of salt marsh,
shops and homes like old friends,
confection-colored clapboard with
peeling paint or fresh—
nothing is strange.
Seems only yesterday we traced this path.

"Didn't I meet you on the beach last summer?"
      the waitress asks,
        "My little boy played trucks with yours."
I remember after only a moment,
suddenly recalling a whole afternoon's conversation
      with a waitress I thought I'd never seen.

                Shift gears
              and a whole world
                comes rushing back,
     as familiar as the sound of your child's laugh.

   I tread the earth,
   feet of clay,
   consuming,

assuming consuming the natural thing to do,
      as if
    there were no other world
    within the mustard seed
    distant
    as my own heart.

Flotsam

The barrel and
heavy timber
studded with sharp
crusted spike,
the water took away.

The rose petals my daughter
yesterday scattered
on the beach
remain.

When Lobstermen Were Lawyers

(We Did Not Walk Uphill Barefoot in the Snow Five Miles
to School)

When lobstermen were lawyers
and kindness was King,
a child could grow up
to be any old thing.
But now times are different,
with fish-folk on Relief
from June until November;
kindness often leads to grief.

When lobstermen were lawyers
and I was the Queen,
there was love and drink for all—
banished were the mean.
Now I boil the water;
now I mop the floor
while the King shops for vittles
and mends the squeaky door.

When lobstermen were lawyers
and poor boys President,
a child could go to college
with scarcely a saved cent.
But that was so long ago—
decades, to be frank—
now you need two working stiffs
and money in the bank.

Pastille:

Bay of Fundy

Runny pastels under water-color sky,
wet reflections left by lace-edged ripples
on a crescent beach.
Six miles for soft walking
where clear water crawls up warm sand.

Sun sets, colors fade,
the long flat line of the horizon
visible only where gloss turns to matte.
Stars prick through the velvet evening,
and the moon smiles up from a dark-daubed silver sea.

Tonight, eight witnesses cross the canvas.
The locals think nothing of this beauty
and envy the city folk
who come to get away from
the blare of our own car alarms.
Here
fishermen never lock their doors,
prefer their fish fried,
and think of lobster as peanut butter—
to be eaten when there's nothing else.

Oasis

On the Delaware,
a delegation of loons,
long absent from this river,
lounges midstream on sunbathed rocks.
One stretches, languidly fans his wings
in the whispery morning breeze,

heedless of the traffic—
hikers, cars, bikers,
beggars, dogs, and dealers—
fanning out on either bank.

Whenever he wishes, he can laugh
and fly back to the Bay of Fundy.
We can, if we wish,
focus our awareness on one pair of dark,
mist-jeweled wings in slant sunlight.

Spring Babble

"She hides in autumn splendor."
This muse I seek?
Unlikely.

Never has she sent me
leafy glories in the nippy air,
golden humus-scented light,
or hoar-frost pumpkins;
but only sparse, dark words
to mark my footsteps where they descend
into winter's desolate cave.

Who speaks this line
here at snow-sleet-rain equinox?
The god I cannot name?
Or one of the voices heard by grandma?

A season of soup-can stars
soars across the senseless screen
of closed eyelids.
I strain to hear
rain's improbable syncopation
on a neighbor's downspout,
as songbirds proclaim
a spring snow only.

Lost

Sunny highway skies
gave way to wispy tendrils of cool fog
that licked our skin as we parked
and headed for the beach.

Beyond the dunes at low tide
the fog was immense,
and soon we were engulfed in eerie whiteness.
We thought to track by sound of breakers
an ocean to tickle our toes,
but sound proved deceptive and led us on and on
along an endless invisible sandscape.
Barely discerning our own limbs, our feet were lost,
and we held hands like children astray in the wood.
I could see your hand, but not you,
nor my own fingers at arm's length.
A disembodied feeling, not fear, but floating wonder
held sway, and I thought of magic
and Tolkien's hobbits wandering the Downs.

Finally we found the dunes again—
surely the highest ones on the beach—
and scrambled, sometimes sliding down, then back up,
laughing and pulling each other,
grasping sea oats and wildflowers to get over the top;
then the small macadam road; and, finally, the car.
In five hundred feet, we emerged as if from a smoky cave
and basked in the sunny heat of the highway.

But wasn't that the year we began to lose each other?

Now, although you're here, I can't quite see you;
and if we bump together in the night,
it's just our bodies groping in the dark.

Like Peter Pan, we've lost our shadows,
and our feelings, disembodied,
remain somewhere in the past,
where white was a beach
unwatered.

Maroon

Rocking in its cradled cup,
the sea tips her wide chalice, sloshes over
at my feet and slakes the waiting sand
as we spin in our mad Sufi dance
        around the sun.

Like a shipwrecked sailor,
I drink with joy
the message of each brine-washed bottle
        that floats my way
and taste the honeyed hope of rescue to come.

But this ungrateful mariner
wants more: to see you on her shore
in gaudy daylight—
personal delivery, daily forecasts, hourly reports
of your remembrance, a rope to pull me in
from my savage state—
a highway through the waves,
a smooth and silvered road home
through moonlit winter deeps
and rock-scarred shallows,
to your front door.

Meanwhile, before my blind eyes,
the very wind carries your word
and your love's in flight
on each passing bird.

FIRE

Best Foot

I know you've got your best foot forward.
It's hard to walk that way.
You think I think you're
some sort of god but
I don't.

I've got my best ear forward,
and what I hear through it
makes my heart beat fast
and shine and cry,
washing away fear and shame and scars,
to blaze in its dark cage
and burn to burst
forth to dance
with your best foot
even to your worst tune.

The Aging Poet

Both legs broken, he
will not accept a crutch.
What could one say,
who would he believe?

Words, once coined like silver
and filigreed to hold fine jewels,
honed and pointed
become sharp enough to fall upon
if one begins to mistake
the hollow of the ear
for the emptiness of song.

Sliding into hopelessness,
descending despairs;
angels weep at such beauty,
mourning our fall.

Palette

If my crayon box stood empty,
I'd want a color like Desire: vermillion.
And one like Hope, greenish-blue, I think.
Joy would be a rainbow swirl with flecks of silver verging
        to a pure white center——the biggest crayon in the box,
        but the hardest to find.
Depression is dun.
Brown for grief.
Potential would be raven——all the fertile colors there,
        fallow; you can't see them for the chaos.
Contentment is sky-blue pink;
Satisfaction, yellow as buttercups in a spring field.
Of violet and gray, Regret is born.
And isn't there a color between fire and smoke
        called Rekindled?

Hyper

Jeckyll to Hyde-child
in a matter of molecules:
excitement crosses synapses
        at the speed of light——
hands strike, throat yowls——
a tesseract of impulse blossoming
        in four dimensions,
while messages of inhibition crawl,
        sometimes founder,
            across that synaptic sea.

"My brain is going too fast,"
he grimaces, hands covering ears
as conscience and regret take their toll,
seep in small fluid jets to muddy the waters,
while the rest of us glare,
shocked or disapproving,
our brains tracking from A to B
like robotic ants, like
trees, too slow-moving to help.

Advanced Attachment

This same desire
that leads us toward the light
keeps us chained in darkness
palpable, now that we can see.

Lured through maze of mirrors,
I hunger for reflections;
the light so strong I shy away,
my aim not true
though I burn with wanting it.
I reach for stars
and find myself enmeshed.
Heading for flame but weighted off with wax,
I gather strength for another pass,
another inside death-spiral
with the candle
leading to the secret passage
behind the wall of flame.

But I fall in love with the candle.

A Glass Darkly

Mirrored in the wet surf sand,
a rainbow halo encircles a blue sun;
and I think of the way
we reflect one another.

You think I'm controlling, inflexible;
but you know it's you
who stands on principle
and tightens the tether,
finessing, pushing, pulling,
counting off the hours and minutes of my days
while I bend and bend and bend.

I think you're harsh and distant,
but I know it's me,
popping in and out of revolving realities
long enough to see what's happening:
who loves me, who needs me,
who's left.
I perform my duties grudgingly
then fly off to greener fantasies
until someone yanks my chain.

And so we weave our images
of tissue, bone, and bulk
inside the orbit of the blue sun.
Who sees my strength?
Who sees your pain?
And who holds the burning mirror for those unmatched?

She Said

You're the only one I can talk to, she said.
They won't even let me say the word cancer.

Sometimes you're so pessimistic I can't be around you, she said.
It's not good for me. I need to be positive.

Well, you made your choice, she said.
You chose to move up north.
You can't be here and there at the same time.

Why can't you just leave me alone? she said.
Why do you keep waking me up to take pills?
Can't you just let me rest?

You moved the clock again, she said.
It was on the other wall this morning.
Everyone keeps playing tricks on me.

You're all spying on me, she said.
I'm going to sue you for invasion of privacy.

Take my jewelry, she said.
Go through it *right now* and take what you want.
Don't let your aunt get any of it.
And don't let her have my bed.

Do I have to put up with that ass? she said.
Get him out of my room.

Don't let your father have any money after I'm gone, she said.
He'll just drink himself to death.

Close the window, she said.
I'll catch a cold.

What are *they* waiting for? she said,
her glare fixed on a blank wall.

You've been good kids, she said.
Everything you'll need is in that file cabinet.

And it was, as she said.

Certain Illnesses

In a family with certain illnesses,
you always put away the sharp knives first
when you open the dishwasher.

You keep the windows locked,
and you know where the first-aid kit is
at all times.

You come home from social events early
if you perchance
forgot to bring the medicine.

In a family with certain illnesses,
you pray a lot,
and you never get to sleep as much as you hoped
or to hope as much as you dreamed.

Civil War

At first it seemed like such a good idea, homey
like iced tea on a freshly painted veranda as wide as Virginia.
Then, thinking only to be kind, we offered to serve the tea,
and suddenly we were slaves,
while the war went on and on.

On both sides at once,
we always found ourselves
on the front lines.

But this is America,
where memories are short
and nothing lasts forever—
            does it?
It's just a phase,
I keep repeating;
it's just my life.
I'm sure there'll be another—
            won't there?

And it's your life, too, both of us
pushing the turning grind
around in dusty circles,
sometimes at cross purposes,
trying to churn the cow's ear
            to a sow's purse,
trying to cover the wagons with bedsheets,
            grease the goats with egg yolks,
            and spin the splintered hay to gold.

Traces

I need to see you gray—
you ghosts: you friends who died too young;
you lovers, lost in the crush of life,
time, place, pressing us on beyond each other's ken;
and especially you,
the unconsummated, who still roams the forest of my heart
      like Robin Hood at 24.

I, who could never imagine adulthood
or remember my own age,
pluck out a single white hair,
frown at the feet of crows, the deepening traces
 of smiles past
and wonder where you are
right now.
I need to see you gray.

Slow Melt

Stars burst forth, burn out, collapse;
glaciers crawl back to their lairs;
forests fall to axe or torch;
floorboards warp while panes of glass
melt down in rotting window frames,
distorting the sky and rippling over the carved Victorian sill,
drip down the wallpaper and pool on the floor.

Still I am
this foolish uncontrolled Self.
I seek to spin my lead to gold,
my hay to halo,
try to wring out perfect love from festering imperfection,
follow silly signs, pursue promises,
devour hope, hear esoteric hints in synchronicity and
try to tear their meanings out
from the context of a multiverse I can't even envision.

Stop the slow simmer, the sullen smolder;
let it burn;
let it all melt down.

Sitting Shiva

Wind up all the clocks,
for Death arrives in a cloak as kind as silk,
where all had expected sackcloth.
And ashes sift on chunks of bone
as mourners promenade
to gentle airs of release.

AIR

Blind Creation

Somewhere where mind trumps matter
we speculate these worlds into being:
Narnia, Middle Earth, Hogwarts,
and all the tiny circles of hell,
little dimensions curled up inside
the fissures of our brains,
the patterns on our pillowcases.

Apostles coin apocalypses,
while fundamentalists draw sure lines
in the sands of their own belief.
Scientists spin theories of evolution,
quantum jumping foam,
galaxies between the atoms
of the bulletin board,
where no angels dance on the heads
of thumbtacks.

The rest of us live in the liminal state
between parallel bars of certainty and grace.
The world is maya, illusion.
But whose illusion is it?

Someone hums the multiverse into being,
and everything else is up to us to perceive.

Some of us trip
over the strip that divides the rug from the linoleum,
so tricky are the textures of life
for those without depth perception.
For us, the world has always been illusion:
foreground turning into background,
lines into stairs,
strangers into friends.
For dyslexics, angles could be angels;
for the nearsighted,

light is neither particle nor wave,
but globe or pinprick;
trees are loose green shapes,
while long green blobs
are forests to lose your own shape in,
then start over, in clay.

Einstein's Not Here

"Spooky action at a distance"
is what the great man said.
Spooky action at a distance
made that hair rise on his head.

Though it wasn't A that got hit
by that proton aimed at B,
still A trembled and exploded,
leaving no one home at C.

Like soulmates across an ocean,
like airwaves to your TV,
could someone else be tuned in
to this thing that I call "me"?

Or is it that I'm there, too,
in the Dreamtime, in the Tao?
Is it that I'm everywhere,
an event that's always Now?

If so, please don't *observe* me——
graven images, and all——
I don't want *my* position fixed,
to hang on someone's wall.

Indulgence in Infrared

Since I hung the pink geranium
on the screened porch

a host of fluttering birds visit,
hover around the screen

like moths around proverbial flame—
delicate wings of sparrow, wren, chickadee, and tiny jeweled
       hummingbirds

who investigate
then fly away disappointed.

It makes me want to paint the yard with scarlet.

I have not worn pink
since I changed my hair.
Someone has been to the Rescue Mission,
I imagine,
a woman of my size but
without my good fortune,
without geraniums or screens,
car or house,
even without kitchen or bath, perhaps,
or a pleasant perch to watch the birds who
may be watching her saunter down the steaming streets
in her glorious pink or ruby garb.

And I think, in my comfort,
about buying a new shirt—
peony pink or carmine.

There are worse legacies
than to be admired by birds.

Mayflies

The mayflies hatch
on Mother's Day,
festoon every screen:
tiny flags of transparent wing
against the sky, glistening in sunlight
as we celebrate with pancakes
a perfect spring day
to live, lust, and die:
a testament to fecundity,
a testament to
brevity.

Happy Ending

"I'm goin' fairy-godmothering,"
Queen Ko-ko-um says with an Attitude.
Putting on her rhinestone crown
and her new black buckle-shoes,
she, with a wave of her ribboned wand
brings all the servants to attention,
changing sweatsuits to ballgowns,
cousins to courtiers,
and brothers to fruit bats
the world over.

She grants herself
Hannah's hair,
Rebecca's best dress,
and Heather's patent leathers.

"Oh, but you're prettier than all of them,"
       we say,
offering her delicacies
from the pantry of Frito-Lay.
"We like you best."

Gap-toothed grin
replaces princess pout and
out come the cornrows
as the crooked crown is flung down.

Snack is served
and all's right with the world.

Northern Cross

He said he'd always wanted to see glaciers and icebergs.
I said I'd always wanted to see palm trees
with clustered coconuts and saw-toothed leaves
whispering in a kiss of wind;
bananas in their natural habitat;
warm blue-green waters, clear as shimmering sky.
Let me go troppo, forget the days of the week,
the points of the compass,
and which side my bread is buttered on!

Alas, it is not I who *has* the bread to butter.
Pass me my parka.

In the Editors' Diner

More metaphor
       is what is wanted.
Your order placed,
       I'll serve it up with slabs of bacon
or piled high on stacks of fluffy buttermilk pancakes.
Your coffee shall be thickened with clotted cream,
for you have lived too long on the watery brew
       of everyday free verse.
You must have pulp in your juice
and gravy to flavor the grit of the slush pile:

And when at last your palate is sated,
when you find yourself somewhat too stuffed
       with superfluous metaphorical meaning,
then will I offer you a tonic of simple verse,
with only a tad of alliteration on toast.

Caged Canary

Longing for the lust of lying
in the grass, with
blades through bare toes,
sun-speckled spring breeze on
cooped-up winter skin,
staring into cerulean sky,
fleecy clouds of childhood's
long summer daze:

We're caged canaries in Rapaccini's garden,
gazing at the beauty of
spring beyond glass,
ozone on the hair-trigger of our reactions,
we no longer take the risk
of basking
while breathing
slow poison in our air and
pain in every grain
of aggravated pollen.

Sing. Sigh. Shriek for the wind.

Sprung:

the seed
the egg
the new life bursting out the cracks
the rose from the bud
the maggot from his casing
the empty nest
the empty tomb
the cross
the baskets of Boadicea
the burned empty human husks
the sacrificial hares
the cloudbursts and the sprouting grain
the black hole sucking in
and blowing out the other side of life
the canvas cleared
the creation begun
the dance of Shiva
the wailing of widows
the return of Persephone
from the dark halls of hell.

Reverie

Light and shadow:
lattice-trace dance
on fallen dogwood blossoms,
breeze-dappled,
deck-barred.

Solid objects sway and dissolve,
reveal spaces between atoms
in the expand-
contract universe
in the slow-living trees,
in the lacework of breathing lungs,
shadow-seeing eyes

until a wren, popping out
of her little house in the dogwood
warbles the world back into being.

Take These Broken Wings

Roused from dark slumbers of hopelessness
through gray panes
of late winter light I groped
to cold kitchen of mid-morning despair, where
I found the source of desperate flapping.
A small brown bird,
following wind through gust-gaped door,
battered itself mindlessly
against the porch screen,
left and right,
in panic blind
to the still-open door behind her.

Clarity came down like rain:
without thought, I raced for the front door,
spurned March mud beneath bare toes,
wind-whipped gown wet with weather.
Propping screen door and
circling round, I,
intent to terrify,
ran headlong at the bird
vainly hurling herself against the screen.

Tricked into turning,
she perceived the true nature of her trap.
Instinctively she flew
through the waiting escape
into the arms of life
and the support of all the unseen lovers
that undergird the Earth.

Twenty years later,
I knew the bird was me
And dared to ask
Who was it set me free?

Chaos Verde

Words like feather dusters
flapping through my brain,
tossing up word salad;
maybe I'm insane.
Heavy with no meaning,
churning dust and peas,
past the point of caring!
Pass the dressing, please.

SPIRIT

Altaring

Leaves for Krishna
mums for Jesus
stones for Ganesh
      who gets the hardest tasks.

Seeking solace
upon the daily altar of my soul
I scatter trinkets for the gods
and navigate by starlight——

babbling like Ophelia
shooting rapids by new moon.

Inventory

Handle the car with grace.
Bundle the candles with saffron ribbon.
Write poems in the margins of the checkbook.
Stand on the table and be heard.
Compute the number of threads in your favorite sweater,
divided by the softness of your husband's hands.
Calculate on an envelope the number of
     full moons in your lifetime.
Count the hair on your head.
Check your purse at the door.
Use your hand to figure the width of
     your soul.
Smile into your pillow.

Call Me Al

Simon says: Start with an image, visual, concrete;
say, "a man walks down the street"——you know the rest.

Say a monk lies in his dark cell waiting for the assassin.
Or a grim-faced man on a dark horse, hair and mane flying
in the wind, charges up a steep hill to rescue you,
        a prisoner with invisible chains.

Say a pretty washerwoman walks down a sunny street
        in feudal London. Her hair is long and flaxen;
specks of mica in the cobblestones dazzle her eyes.
        She is happy.

Or you're a man in love with a dark-haired peasant girl
        in a hayloft.
        You want her so much it hurts.

Say the little wife on the prairie lies awake listening
to the cold wind and for the sound of soft footfalls,
        fearing death at a young age.

Say you climb into vintage clothes and slip back along your
own lifeline to warn those you love.
        But not one of them will listen to you.

Say the assassin is silhouetted in the doorway,
and the monk—instead of waking with a scream—
        finally dies.

And say an angel named Al pulls you back to the present
in nothing but your historical lover's Chinese silk bathrobe—

        just in time for Christmas.

What do all these people have in common?
Some mysteries are too deep for us,
        too subliminal even for the angels.
Like the difference between
created and creator:
        which of them really walks down this street?

Splintered Symphony

Fields of red-tipped weeds,
buttercups,
clover,
purple marsh iris,
rustling berry bushes,
ruffled evergreens,
startled doves;
legions of lives,
your soul,
mine,
whitecaps on the gulf between:
splinters of God,
fractured deity,
each emanating its piece of the Light;
emitting its own tones,
sweet and sour.

Through all this white noise,
in my heart's old radio,
I strain to hear the conductor.

Sometimes when I least expect,
sunlight glints off a baton.

The Listing Wife

For the new year I began making lists
to organize my life
and so my husband could stop
dropping hints about
        Alzheimers,
                Prozac, or
                        Ritalin,
making me wonder if I was in the
sixty percent of Americans
who will this year turn themselves in
as victims of Adult A.D.D.

But living by the list has its limits,
leaving one flustered
when too many things unlisted
hitch a ride on the week,
or when you discover that a child
can go unbathed for five days
because you forgot to write: "Bath."

An angel appeared.
Given the state of my mind,
I wasn't surprised, except for the wings.
Not knowing if angel etiquette had changed
        over the centuries,
I dropped uncertainly to my knees.
I thought wings were invented by European artists,
and even though I didn't say so,
s/he smiled and the wings vanished.

"Throw away your list,"
the angel said.
"Here's a new one."

I'd seen it before:
second Book of Moses.
Terrified,
I still had to ask.
"What's this," I squeaked,
"about 'other gods before me'?
Are there other gods?"

The smile remained, benificent,
warm like your grandmother's
when she was proud of you
or Yogananda
in that photo taken
a few hours before he died,
startling everyone in Forest Lawn
by beaming that way for several months,
smile fading last, like the Cheshire Cat's.

Emboldened, I went on,
"and this bit about 'Honor thy father and thy mother
so that *you* may have long life'——
is that about karma or what?"

But the angel was not there——
not that it "disappeared"
or faded away like Yogananda's smile,
simply
not there.
And I held a page, which,
on further investigation,
had been torn from the King James Bible downstairs——
the one given to me by the Kentland Baptist Sunday School,
where they scared me as a six-year-old
into having nightmares about horned
"Roaming Catholics" who led the way to hell.

Some of this is falsehood,
but things almost as strange have occurred.

Over the years
I have traveled through paths of religions thick as trees,
and deserts of existential atheism
where to be lame is to curse a crutch
and pain wrings denouncement of opiates from the writhing
until there are no words left worth saying.

Whenever darkness was most intense,
a single silver thread
dangled before me:
      a bird,
           a book,
                a song,
                    a tattered homeless woman,
                    laughing and shouting
                    my most secret password at me—
                        a thousand
                            impossible
                                coincidences.

Let me pretend for a moment that I Believe—
      oh, the wondrous things that start to happen!
Let me pretend for a moment that love surrounds me,
that happiness falls like cherry blossoms on my upturned face—
      oh, I can live!
Give me those crutches
and by God how I will walk!
Let me dream of angels
and the very air will flutter and sing.

Next you will smile, strained, sardonic,
listing the virtues of lithium.

Then will I grin, sheepish,
and smiling like Ophelia say:
    Snake oil for the deaf,
    Thalidomide for the blind,
    Make a list.
    You've got yours and
    I've got mine.

The Hindu Quaker

The simple Quaker part
knows the clearest path,
and yet
so sensory am I
that the path of exotics——
sensual Hindu gods
entice me
with their beauty and their smiles,
their kind embracing eyes.
I have heard them call me,
have heard them speak,
felt them laugh,
basked in their warmth
until my native faith starts to seem strange and cold.

More alien than Krishna and Ganesh
is a tragic Aryan avatar,
summed up in the moment of sacrifice,
worshipped in bloody sacrifice,
frozen in solemn sacrifice
or innocent infancy,
message forgotten,
framed between the bookends of birth and burial.

I long to see a graven image
with no resemblance to a German ascetic
or to a portrait from Renaissance art,
but like a Middle Eastern carpenter
so little different from his fellows,
so unexceptional that he needed to be
pointed out for Pilate, to be
singled out by Judas' kiss.

And most of all, I need to see him smile.
Even a man of sorrows
must smile sometimes.
Surely walking on water involves *some* whimsy.

Meditation

Stiff and distracted
I struggle to find myself,
to settle down
in the garden of my soul.

Mantras come and mantras go,
my mind a nervous monkey
while intrusions of synapse and sound
fire in and around me.

Urban pioneers,
me and the monkey,
fending off phones, doorbells,
car alarms, muscle cramps,
lists and forgotten errands,
coming around again to

batter at the walls of the
inner sanctum:
i-am-spirit-let-me-in!

Sit still, listen to the slowing heart
    ta-dum
        ta-dum
            ta-dum....

The monkey turns, dog-like,
and settles down to sleep;
    we are one.

The barriers don't drop but
finally, I melt through,
like slipping into someone's arms:

    home at last.

Recycled

The galaxies are flowers in your field
and I a molecule on a grain of pollen.
                Inhale.
I'll come in and metabolize again
through grace
and be one with you——
perhaps a cell of your liver,
pretending for years that you don't exist,
but grateful
nonetheless
that you don't imbibe too much
for me to process.

Some Grace

I close my eyes
and see the lacy gray veins
as an overlay on the red of my eyelids,
like a translucent slice of cantaloupe.

Higher,
images bob and disappear, fragments
form and dissolve.
I am only just beginning to learn to see.

I think of my little daughter
mistaking a donkey for a dog,
a plum for a ball,
learning to put names
to the shapes of this material world;
learning to filter out the background noise
and focus on sounds
that will guide her to comprehend
        this place
well enough to move through it
with some grace.

The Gift

There is always a pillow for love's head;
there is always sunlight
to gild the side of his face.
Whatever the folly of love's eye,
it is always better to love than not.

Forage

Even the plants have more faith.
We bruit our brains but scarce perceive
the pattern of a day
much less a weave of weeks,
a history, a family, or a lifetime.
Daisies track the sun across the sky
and sleep away the dark, enfolded in cool confidence.
We toss in troubled slumbers,
doubting light,
mistaking manna for luck or fluke,
suspicious of our outer senses
and inner compass too.

Here, lost in the thicket of our own devising,
I have left my self to forage in wonder
at the fortitude of foxglove,
the grace of common grass.

About the Author

Photo by Amy D. Goldstein, Leichner Studios.

Denise Thompson-Slaughter is a writer and editor whose poems have appeared in numerous literary journals. In 2000, her poem "Haiku for Willie" won the J. Franklin Dew award from the Poetry Society of Virginia. Born in Washington, D.C. Denise has lived in Maryland, New Jersey, California, Indiana, and New York. With a B.A. in English from Rutgers University, she has worked for many years as an editor, both academic and freelance. She is currently the managing editor of *Reviews in American History* at the University of Rochester. Denise lives with her husband, two teenaged children, and various pets in western New York, where she is polishing up a book on parapsychology and toying with the idea of writing fiction.

www.ingramcontent.com/pod-product-compliance
Lightning Source LLC
Chambersburg PA
CBHW052109070526
44584CB00017B/2399